Getting Creative with

FAB LAB™

Creating with
LASER
CUTTERS
and
ENGRAVERS

MARY-LANE KAMBERG

rosen publishing's
rosen central®

for Harper Falls

Published in 2017 by The Rosen Publishing Group, Inc.
29 East 21st Street, New York, NY 10010

Library of Congress Cataloging-in-Publication Data

Names: Kamberg, Mary-Lane, 1948– author.
Title: Creating with Laser Cutters and Engravers / Mary-Lane Kamberg.
Description: First edition. | New York : Rosen Publishing, 2017. | Series: Getting creative with Fab Lab | Includes bibliographical references and index.
Identifiers: LCCN 2016027240 | ISBN 9781499465044 (library bound)
Subjects: LCSH: Lasers—Juvenile literature. | Laser beam cutting—Juvenile literature. | Engraving—Juvenile literature. | Makerspaces—Juvenile literature.
Classification: LCC TA1682 .K36 2017 | DDC 621.36/6—dc23
LC record available at https://lccn.loc.gov/2016027240

Manufactured in China

Contents

Introduction

Let's make something! Anything at all. Out of almost anything. Using easy-to-use, computer-controlled fabrication machines.

Today, individuals can design, invent, and create new products the way big business manufacturers do. New availability of small versions of equipment once limited to use in huge factories lets everyone produce whatever he or she can think of.

Want a new necklace? A toy? An alarm clock you have to wrestle with to prove you're awake? How about a machine controlled by a Lego set that makes other machines? A solar turbine? Parts for NASA satellites? Artificial knees? You can do it all in a Fab Lab.

In fact, anyone can make almost anything in a Fab Lab almost anywhere in the world. A Fab Lab is a small-scale, community-based workshop with computer-controlled machines that individuals can use for free or at a small cost to make things. This type of manufacturing is known as personal digital fabrication.

Fab Labs are the shop classes of the new millennium. One of the machines students can learn to use in a Fab Lab is the laser cutter. Laser cutters use an intense beam of light to cut or engrave a piece of wood, acrylic, glass, leather, or other materials. Mild steel, stainless steel, and other metals can be engraved (but not

Fab Labs are found all over the world. This one, located in the International Centre for Theoretical Physics (ICTP) in Trieste, Italy, features a 3D printer, along with other personal fabrication machinery.

cut) only if they are anodized or coated with LMM6000 CerMark/ TherMark laser marking ink or a similar product.

The design is created on a computer, and the computer guides the laser to produce the design. A laser cutter is just one of many machines bringing high-tech manufacturing to individuals and their communities.

Chapter
ONE

THE SCOOP ON FAB LABS

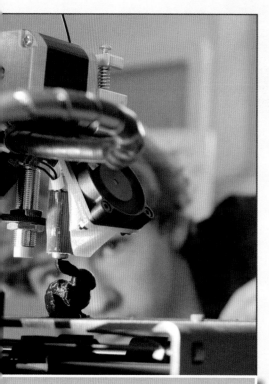

In Fab Labs, students get a chance to imagine, experiment, and make things while also learning high-tech skills that they will be able to use in the future.

Fab Lab is a place where anyone can learn about and use the latest technology to make goods for personal use or to solve community-wide (or even global) problems. It's a workshop filled with high-tech manufacturing machines that cut and bend a wide variety of materials. And almost anyone can use them. A Fab Lab is also a place where participants help each other learn, while working to make something for free or at a low cost.

Some use Fab Labs for artistic creations. Others make parts to repair bicycles or other equipment. Still others make copies of objects

FAB LAB OR MAKERSPACE: WHAT'S THE DIFFERENCE?

Makerspaces and Fab Labs are both community workshops that offer public access to equipment for personal manufacturing. The main difference between the two is similar to comparing a mom-and-pop hamburger stand to a McDonald's. A makerspace is independent, while a Fab Lab is like a franchise.

Although the term "makerspace" became loosely associated with *Make:* magazine when Dale Dougherty founded the periodical in 2011, it has been around since at least 2005. Makerspaces are almost-always-open places where anyone can make anything from scratch out of any material. The spaces house a variety of manufacturing tools for both hobbyists and professional craftsmen. They're usually set up like for-profit businesses and use membership fees to pay for machinery and other costs.

Fab Lab is a trademarked name for a network of community workspaces that include a core set of equipment, software, and tools in a specified space—usually between 1,000 and 2,000 square feet (93 to 186 square meters). Although the Massachusetts Institute of Technology (MIT) exercises little or no supervision of individual Fab Labs, the MIT principles define them. They are often run by nonprofit organizations and open to the public either free or at a low cost. They also include a curriculum to teach children and adults basic introductions to engineering and design so they can make objects from scratch.

already in existence. Fab Labs also provide an environment where people can invent new products to solve problems for themselves or their communities.

Where It Began

The Fab Lab program began around 2005 at the Massachusetts Institute of Technology's (MIT's) Center for Bits and Atoms in MIT's Media Lab. Neil Gershenfeld, an MIT professor, wanted to explore the relationship between the content of information and how it can be represented as a physical object. He teamed with MIT's Grassroots Invention Group and got a grant from the National Science Foundation to buy manufacturing machinery with the latest technology to make anything of almost any size.

Once the machines were in place, however, Gershenfeld found himself spending more time teaching students how to use the machines than actually using them for research. He started a class called How to Make (Almost) Anything. He expected a few research students to sign up. However, hundreds of students were interested in the class—not to do research, but to make things—even though they had little or no technical background.

One requirement of the grant was outreach. To satisfy this kind of requirement, most grant recipients offer classes or produce a website. Instead, Gershenfeld chose to create public-access workspaces and make the high-tech tools he was using available to ordinary people. The first Fab Lab was opened in Boston's inner city. Soon, others opened in Bhopal, India; Sekondi-Takoradi, Ghana; Soshanguve, South Africa; and northernmost Norway. In a TED talk, Gershenfeld said, "The real opportunity is to harness the inventive power of the world to locally design and produce solutions to local problems."

Neil Gershenfeld, director of the Massachusetts Institute of Technology's Center for Bits and Atoms, got the idea for Fab Labs to satisfy an outreach requirement of a grant from the National Science Foundation.

As of 2016, according to the Fab Labs World Map, at least 660 Fab Labs worldwide let individuals design and create products for their own use or to help solve local and global problems. They're found in high schools, colleges, and community centers on every continent, in bustling urban communities and remote villages. And they're making a difference in people's lives.

What's in a Fab Lab?

MIT's Center for Bits and Atoms has listed equipment and other supplies needed in official Fab Labs. However, specific Fab Lab equipment may vary in different locations. Not all Fab Labs have everything on the list, and some have additional machines. At the least, however, Fab Labs need computers and monitors with supporting software. They also need machines from specific manufacturers. The list includes an Epilog laser cutter and ventilation system, a Roland milling machine, a Roland vinyl cutter, a ShopBot closed-loop router and dust collector, and a 3D printer from 3D Systems,

Stratasys-Objet, EnvisionTEC, Makerbot Industries, or Ultimaker, along with basic hand tools.

If you're new to a Fab Lab, a great place to start is with the laser cutter. It's one of the easiest machines to use and the most popular in most labs. The only negative is the odor the cutter produces as it works. That's why any Fab Lab with a laser

STEAM AND FAB LAB: HOW DO THEY OVERLAP?

In tomorrow's world, even more than today's, employers will seek workers with the knowledge and skills to gather and evaluate information and solve problems. That's why today's educators emphasize science, technology, engineering, arts and design, and math, also known as STEAM education. STEAM focuses on a mixture of the disciplines, rather than treating them as separate subjects. Also, instead of relying on theory, STEAM uses real-world applications of these sciences. STEAM also encourages combining experiences in school with other experiences outside the school environment.

Fab Labs support these goals with hands-on experience, combining technology with artistic design and engineering principles in pursuit of new products. While participants may begin using a Fab Lab with little or no technical knowledge, brief instruction on the use of computer-driven tools lets them get right to work creating, inventing, and building. In the process they learn skills that will serve them well in pursuing crafting hobbies, as well as future employment.

cutter needs a ventilation system—to remove the smells and any smoke produced by too much heat. You can use the laser cutter to engrave such materials as wood, acrylic, painted brass, and anodized aluminum. Anodizing is a coating that protects the metal. A laser cutter won't engrave bare metal, but it will engrave the paint or anodized coating.

Computer Numerical Control (CNC) machines use computers to control machine tools. Fab Labs must contain a CNC router. A router is a power tool guided by a computer file. Routers are used in carpentry for making grooves in wood for joints and moldings. This machine is used in woodworking to make furniture, musical instruments, signs, and even boats! Working with wood creates sawdust, so the lab will also have a dust collector to attach to the router to remove any excess.

One of the most fun machines in a Fab Lab is the 3D printer. First available in 1980, 3D printers have been used in industrial manufacturing for decades. Today, however, smaller, more affordable printers bring the technology to personal

A milling machine, like this "mini" created by students at the Massachusetts Institute of Technology's Center for Bits and Atoms, works by removing material to create images and messages.

fabrication. You start with a virtual design created with a 3D modeling program or 3D scanner. The design is saved in a computer-aided design (CAD) file. Software creates narrow slices of the design about the width of a human hair. The design is then manufactured with an additive process. Instructed by the computer, the process creates one layer of the final object and then adds each consecutive layer.

While 3D printers add material to an object, a milling machine takes away material, particularly wood, steel, or other metals and solids. Using a CAD file, you can carve out your choice of designs using a CNC mill.

The vinyl cutter rounds out the range of Fab Lab machinery. A vinyl cutter is a computer-controlled machine with a sharp blade. It's used to cut out shapes from sheets of thin plastic for signs, stickers, and other uses.

Fab Labs may also contain plasma cutters and water jet cutters. Plasma is an ionized state of matter that conducts electricity. A plasma cutter uses a plasma cutting torch to remove material from electrically conductive metals. A water jet cutter uses water under high pressure to cut wood, rubber, or other soft materials. A water jet cutter may also use a mixture of water and abrasives to cut such hard materials as granite or metal.

In addition to these tools, Fab Labs offer technical support and shared knowledge among users.

Chapter
TWO

WHAT'S A LASER CUTTER, AND HOW DOES IT WORK?

If you want to cut or engrave wood, acrylic, glass, mild steel, stainless steel, aluminum plates, painted brass, some plastics, or many other materials, a laser cutter is the Fab Lab machine to use. A laser cutter can cut tiny holes and detailed shapes. It also delivers detailed images for engraving. It can engrave fine lines on almost anything you'd like to personalize: award plaques, drinking glasses, iPhones, laptops, and more.

"Laser" stands for light amplification by stimulated emission of radiation. A carbon dioxide (CO_2) laser cutter—the kind found in a Fab Lab—cannot cut metals, but can engrave them. In a typical CO_2 laser, the infrared light beam has a diameter of about three-quarters of an inch (1.9 centimeters), which is then focused to a single pinpoint. A resonator is a device that moves

Epilog Laser manufactures the "Legend" CO_2 laser cutters and engravers found in many Fab Labs and makerspaces around the world. The line includes the small format Epilog Mini 18 and Helix models.

electromagnetic radiation back and forth; it creates the beam of light. The beam then travels along a path directed by one or more mirrors through a nozzle bore to the object being cut or engraved. Compressed gas also travels through the nozzle bore to provide the force of the beam.

On a laser cutter used in a Fab Lab, the cutting head moves over the material according to the programmed shape in the CAD file. Accuracy is achieved by controlling the height of the end of the nozzle above the material being cut. The machine cuts by melting, burning, or vaporizing parts of the selected object. A laser beam creates intense heat, so it's not a good choice for vinyl or PVC (polyvinyl chloride), a synthetic plastic polymer. However, you can use a laser cutter for ABS and polycarbonate. ABS (acrylonitrile-butadiene-styrene) is an inexpensive engineering plastic. Polycarbonate is a strong, heat-resistant synthetic resin.

STAYING SAFE WITH A LASER CUTTER

As with any power tool, a laser cutter can be dangerous. You can be injured or start a fire. So always read the laser cutter manual and complete training before operating. And, always be sure you have a responsible, qualified adult supervising the Fab Lab. If you're not sure what to do, ask for help.

Potential dangers include:

- **Fire** Many materials, especially wood and paper, are flammable if cut at the wrong speed or power. In general, the higher the power, the higher the heat produced. Be sure a CO_2 fire extinguisher is nearby, and know how to use it. Never leave a laser cutter unattended while it is running.

- **Fumes** Some materials release smoke or dangerous gases when heated. The machine should be used along with a ventilator to clear unwanted fumes. Be sure that the filter is on during cutting, and keep the cutter's lid closed for a while after the job is finished.

- **Trapping** When working inside the cutting area or when the lid is open, take care that hands, hair, or clothing remain free of the machinery. Before closing the lid, check to be sure nothing has fallen into the machine.

- **Burns/Light** Normally, the laser is safe within the machine. It should automatically stop when the lid is open (but don't count on it). Looking through the

(continued on the next page)

> **(continued from the previous page)**
>
> top window is safe while the machine is cutting, but don't try to observe it in any other way. Keep all side panels closed and locked whenever the machine is plugged in.

Step by Step

Once you have a laser cutter to use and the material you plan to cut or etch, you'll need a computer and monitor with vector graphics software. One that's commonly used is Corel Draw. It includes clip-art images and lots of fonts to help you design your Fab Lab projects. (The machinery should be compatible with the Corel Draw version you use. Older machines may not work well with newer software.)

Next choose power, speed, and frequency settings. Power measures the rate energy flows, expressed in watts. It's the amount of energy applied to the laser while it's in use. Speed is how fast the laser beam moves when cutting or engraving. A slow speed means the laser will hover longer over the same spot creating a deeper cut. A faster speed creates shallower cuts as the laser moves across the material being engraved.

Each material requires its own power and speed adjustments. For example, different woods react differently to the laser beam. Different thicknesses of acrylic do the same. Also, laser cutters themselves have different wattage settings. That means the same power level may produce different results from different machines. Always check the laser cutter manufacturer's manual for advice. And test the material before trying to cut or engrave it.

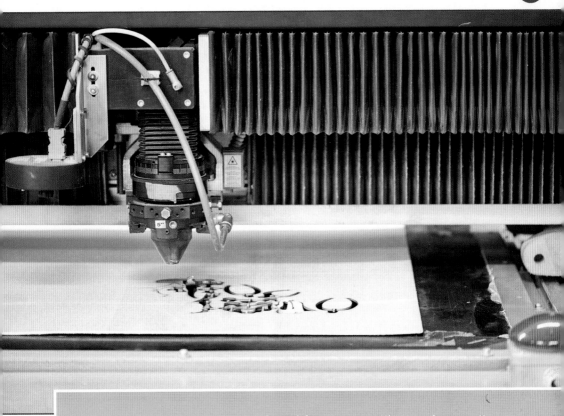

Depending on the power, speed, and frequency settings, a laser cutter can engrave, cut an outline, or cut out holes in a wide variety of materials.

When you work on a project, record the settings that produced desired results on each type of material. Use the same settings when working on future projects with the same material.

Laser cutters use two different cutting techniques. Raster works like an inkjet printer and is usually used for engraving things. The laser beam turns on and off, producing a pre-set number of dots per inch (dpi), often in the thousands. The higher the dpi, the darker the engraved area will look. You can use a raster for all kinds of images.

Vector cutting is used to cut things out. In vector mode, the laser beam stays on until it traces the entire image. It cuts

A high-pressure water jet cutting machine cuts like a laser cutter, but uses water instead of a light beam. The water jet cutter often is used to make machine parts and cut hard material like granite.

more like a knife than a printer. For vector cutting, you need to set the beam's frequency. Depending on the desired effect, vector frequency should be set between ten and five thousand pulses per inch. For vector cutting, you need a clean outline for the laser to trace.

Test Cuts

Now the process moves to the computer. Start the software program, and select the file you want to print. Be sure the size of the design fits the bed of the laser cutter. If not, resize it. Using the corner formed by the rulers as a guide, drag the image to the printable image area.

Click File >Print. Then click on Properties. Choose the cutting technique (raster or vector) and set the speed. For testing in raster, you need a lower resolution (dpi) that prints faster than for actual cutting. Testing a vector image takes additional formatting depending on what material you are using. After that, go to Print and select your preferences. You're almost ready to print.

However, it's a good idea to test your settings on a sample piece of the material you're using.

Turn on the laser and open the lid. Place your material in the machine. If you're going to do a test print, cover the material with blue painter's tape. This type of tape is easy to remove without leaving a sticky residue. Or, you can tape a piece of paper over the area.

Now adjust the bed so the laser won't actually touch the material. For a test, leave the lid open on the machine. (It won't print with the lid open.) Press the test button. The head will travel along the material, so you can tell if you have placed the material correctly. Make any necessary adjustments.

On the computer, in File >Print, select a high speed and low power (0–15 percent). Next, click Auto Focus. The machine will move itself the correct distance from the material. Be sure the exhaust fan is running. (For vector cutting, turn on the air compressor.) Push the Go button on the machine. Check the results and make any changes. Remove the tape or paper from the material, and close the cutter lid. Press OK on the computer to start printing.

Stay with the machine until the printing ends. Wait a few minutes to let the ventilator remove smoke and any gases before retrieving your finished project. Turn off the machine. Clean the laser cutter according to the manufacturer's instructions after each use.

Chapter
THREE

WHAT'S IT LIKE IN A FAB LAB?

If you've never been to a Fab Lab, expect to feel welcomed. Fab Labs are open to everyone, although there may be minimal fees to participate. Fab Labs associated with public schools and colleges often are free to enrolled students and instructors, with memberships available to community members. You'll likely find a mix of instructors, students, and artists working alongside you.

Fab Labs are noisy. Some equipment is noisier than others. So, depending on who is using what, even one participant can almost drown out the rest of the sound in the room. You might be the only person in the lab. Or, people might be using some or all of the other machines at the same time as you.

Fab Labs are clean. Participants and lab supervisors take care to see that work areas are free from dirt, waste materials, and clutter. A ventilator on a laser cutter removes smoke and

A Fab Lab like this one at the Alaska Federation of Natives Annual Convention in Fairbanks, Alaska, can accommodate many users at once. However, you might have to wait in line for a particular machine.

odors from engraving and cutting. A dust collector attached to a CDC router removes dust particles as the cutting takes place.

Fab Labs are supervised. A technician who operates the lab on a daily basis acts as a teacher/guide for participants. He or she usually has a mechanical or electrical engineering background or a manufacturing background, and/or electronics and programming skills. A good example of this kind of person is a high school teacher who has led robotics competition design teams or classes. Others include teachers with training in the arts, architecture, or industrial arts.

The technician's job is to maintain equipment and supplies, as well as train participants on the software and machinery in the lab. This person also runs tours of the facility and designs programs for schools and other community groups. He or she serves as a mentor, guiding participants with their projects. The technician documents the material, power, speed, and frequency used for participants' projects to use as a resource for others. Ask him or her for advice and technical assistance. However, don't expect this person to make your project for you.

In addition, a technical support person may be available to maintain the computers, as well as the networking and internet

WHAT'S YOUR ROLE?

If you plan on using a Fab Lab, you have some responsibilities, too. These include the following:

- Never endanger other people or damage the machines.
- Learn all the safety rules as they relate to each machine (such as using a ventilation system with a laser cutter).
- Know all emergency procedures.
- Know how to find and operate the fire extinguisher.
- Keep your own workspace clean and free of clutter.
- Help clean the machines you use, as well as the rest of the lab.
- Always look for suggestions to improve the Fab Lab.

access. If many of the users are entrepreneurs who plan to start businesses, the lab may also have a full-time designer or engineer to assist in the design of their products.

What You Need

Before you enter a Fab Lab, it helps if you have a little background in using computers and power tools. If you have neither, the lab technician can help you with basic use of the Fab Lab computers and other equipment.

However, try to have reasonable expectations. Start with a relatively easy project like engraving text on wood. Don't try

Teens at a makerspace in Detroit, Michigan, work together with adult advisers to build a radio using fabrication machinery. Experience working with 21st-century equipment may lead to new hobbies or even careers.

to build a scale model of the Eiffel Tower for your first (or second!) project. Start small and build on your skills. The technician is there to help you, but you should need less help on the same machine with each consecutive visit.

You can learn to use a laser cutter and other equipment in the Fab Lab itself. However, for complicated projects, you might want to take a credit or noncredit class to learn basic design or drafting or how to draw on a computer to be able to create designs for your projects. You might also look for a class in the type of software the Fab Lab uses. In addition to Corel Draw, some labs might use Illustrator, Auto Cut, or Rhino Cut.

Once you've decided on your project, you need to provide your own materials. Some are more expensive than others, so start with budget-friendly ones. Wood is probably easiest to start with, and engraving is easier than cutting. Each project will have a number of variables though. For example, the kind of wood and its thickness determine the difficulty and the settings you use.

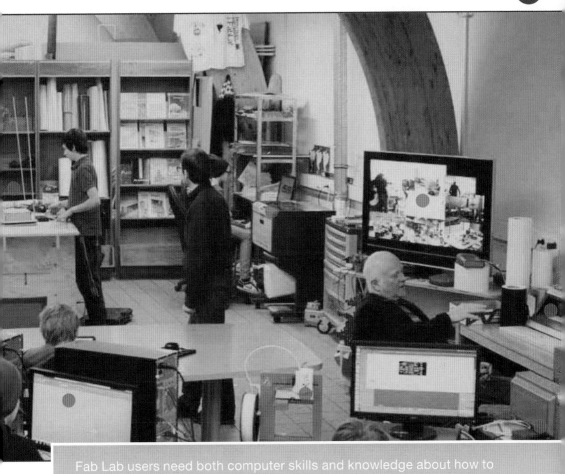

Fab Lab users need both computer skills and knowledge about how to use the fabrication equipment. A lab supervisor or lab technician can offer instruction and advice.

What You Need to Know

To find a Fab Lab near you, enter "Fab Lab" and your city in your web browser, or contact the Fab Foundation for a list of member labs. You can find Fab Labs in community centers, community colleges, and traditional colleges and universities. You may also find classes in middle schools or high schools or schools of higher

DON'T CUT THIS!

While laser cutters can engrave or cut a wide variety of materials, some materials cannot be used at all or only with great care. Here are some to stay away from:

- **Normal plywood** has glue that is not compatible. (However, you can use "laser ply.")
- **MDF (medium-density fiberboard)** is made with either hardwood or softwood fibers, wax, and resin. MDF clogs filters and produces a bad odor.
- **LaserMDF** produces less filter-clogging gunk than MDF, but still is not recommended.
- **PVC (polyvinyl chloride)/vinyl** releases chlorine gas that produces toxic hydrochloric acid when mixed with moisture in the air.
- **Silicone** is nearly impossible to cut with a laser except in thicknesses up to only 0.08 inches (2 millimeters), and it chars easily.
- **Black Delrin acetal** contains carbon black, a possible toxin.
- **Teflon** is also toxic.
- **GPPS/Polystyrene/HIPS** in foam form is highly flammable. (However, you can use these materials in solid sheet form.)

Other materials to avoid include nylon, polythene/polyethylene, LEXAN polycarbonate, carbon fiber, and fiberglass. Materials to use only with great care because of fire risk include paper/card, tissue, polypropylene, and white Delrin acetal.

education that use local Fab Labs or have their own machinery. Visit the Fab Lab's website for information about hours and whether you need to take an orientation or safety class before using. Check for special programs or classes the lab may offer.

You're also expected to know which materials can and cannot be used in a laser cutter. Some that are good to use include wood, cork, glass, acrylic/Perspex, and slate. Ask your lab technician first before using any materials in a laser cutter.

Of course, you also must know the lab's general safety rules, as well as rules for the laser cutter itself. You don't usually need safety glasses to use the laser cutter. However, your lab may require all participants to wear them at all times in the lab. Ask whether your lab provides protective eyewear or whether you should bring your own.

To work with a laser cutter, you need to know how to operate the particular machine you'll be using. The lab technician can teach you. You might also want to read the manufacturer's manual. Ask to see it.

For each project, keep a record that includes the material and settings used. Bring this record with you on each visit. You may want to make another object just like the first, or try some variations. Your record will be a valuable tool to help you make adjustments for more projects.

Chapter
FOUR

STARTER PROJECTS AND BEYOND

Creating projects with a laser cutter is easy if you under-stand some of the advantages the machinery offers. Laser cutters cut and engrave with precision. They're accurate down to thousandths of an inch or centimeter. If you measure carefully, you'll make parts that fit together well. Another advantage is the fact that laser cutters can cut the same shape multiple times, yielding identical objects with the same measurements. They can also easily cut and engrave intricate shapes. Your designs are limited only by your imagination.

Laser cutting is faster than other digital fabrication methods found in a Fab Lab. It can also be faster than similar jobs performed using traditional woodworking tools, machines, and methods. That means you can make quick changes to your design and make new, better products. Chances are your first attempt at a new project won't turn out exactly as you hope. The good news is you can make another, improved version. Before you begin, understand your own skill level when creating expectations for the project. At the same time, be willing to stretch and try new methods.

Getting Started

For the best chance of success in a Fab Lab, consult the lab technician for advice. Start small: make a sign by engraving words, a picture, or another design on one side of a piece of wood. With practice you can advance to three-dimensional sculptures and work with a rotary attachment to engrave glasses, bottles, jars, and other rounded objects. The manufacturer of Epilog laser cutters offers many suggestions to get you started. Or, search for "laser cutter projects" in your web browser.

Simple engraving projects are best at first. Start with durable materials, such as bamboo. A laser cutter used on this wood produces nice depth and contrast. Look for ready-made products and add your own designs. For instance, buy a bamboo tissue box and make it your own by engraving each side with the laser cutter. Or, look for a bamboo iPad case you can personalize with your name or monogram.

Stick with engraving for a while and try different materials. Engrave a copy of your high school diploma on a wooden plaque. Or, get a bamboo cutting board or mahogany serving tray and engrave it with a favorite quotation or image. Cork engraves well. Purchase cork tiles and add your own designs for wall décor or bulletin boards, or make a set of coasters. Try engraving on slate or ceramic tiles prepared for use with lasers. Acrylic is a

Using a laser cutter to engrave a design on a ready-made wooden object like this cutting board is a good Fab Lab project for a beginner.

little harder to work with, but you can produce nice results with practice. Ask for help from the lab technician.

If you're interested in fashion, use a laser cutter for products using fabrics such as silk, leather, neoprene, polyester, and cotton. Engrave a picture or saying on a polyester and cotton apron, denim tote bag, tightly woven cotton placemat, or microfiber throw pillow. Or, engrave your nickname or favorite sports team on the durable canvas found on Converse sneakers.

FABRICS FOR "FASHIONISTAS"

Some designers of high fashion clothing have jumped on the laser cutter bandwagon, using lasers to cut out exotic designs on fabric dresses, purses, hats, shoes, suede coats, and more. Alexander McQueen, a British fashion designer known for unusual and experimental work, was among the first to use industrial laser cutters to make dresses with price tags higher than $5,000. His laser-cut leather dress was originally priced at $6,895, and his laser-cut high-heeled booties made from kid leather sold for $1,275.

He inspired other high-end designers such as John Galliano, whose fall 2016 collection included laser-cut denim, and Jean Paul Gaultier, who designed a rayon-wool blend tailored jacket with a laser-cut embroidered lapel. He also featured a laser-cut silver dress worn by Gossip vocalist Beth Ditto in his spring 2011 collection.

Today, ready-to-wear brands also sell clothing made from fabrics cut with lasers. For example, Burberry, a British brand known for making trench coats, offered a floral and mesh lace dress for $1,595 and perforated leather sandals for $525 on its website in 2016. You can also find laser-cut clothing at Topshop, ASOS, and Forever 21 for a more affordable price.

Moving On

Once you've worked with engraving projects, try some that use the vector setting on the laser cutter to cut out shapes or make holes in things. You can make holiday ornaments from alder wood. The laser cutter will engrave the surface and then cut out the shapes, as well as a hole for the ornament hook.

You can also make a hanging mobile for a child's room out of one-eighth-inch- (0.32-cm-) thick alder or walnut with durable thread or cord from a craft store for hanging the shapes. You can make decorative placemats out of felt by designing patterns to cut out in a lacework form or by using circular holes. Using both

A laser cutter rotary attachment lets you engrave or cut such rounded objects as drumsticks, drinking glasses, jars, or lampshades.

the raster and vector settings, make your own birdhouse out of two 24-inch by 4-inch pieces (61-cm by 10-cm) of one-quarter-inch- (0.63-cm-) thick painted basswood. Engrave "shingles" on the roof. Next, try using the rotary attachment on the laser cutter. It lets you turn rounded items, such as wooden drumsticks, drinking glasses, or jars.

Some laser-happy foodies have taken to engraving fruits and vegetables with laser cutters. They've etched pictures on eggplants, entire paragraphs on zucchini, and quotations on apples. They've also made gingerbread houses and layered laser-cut peach pie top crust in the shape of leaves. One pancake lover created a Spirograph design cooked into batter that had been poured into an empty circle cut out of a piece

FUTURE OF FRUIT

Fruit growers in the European Union (EU) have found a practical use for laser cutters. They have replaced the stickers commonly found on fruit in grocery stores with laser markings for price look-up (PLU) codes and bar codes that identify the price and origin of the produce.

The EU first banned use of iron oxides and hydroxides to coat citrus, melons, and pomegranates to give more contrast to laser etching. However, thanks to a three-year-long lobbying effort by Spain's Laser Food, a "new generation" labeling company, the EU lifted the ban on June 23, 2013.

The ruling does not require laser etching by growers, but simply allows it.

of wood. Heat and engraving techniques from the laser cutter cooked the food.

Your Fab Lab may not allow food in its laser cutter, so before trying any exotic materials, do consult the lab technician. He or she may be willing to try it as long as it won't damage the machine or leave behind anything that could rot or attract bugs.

Amazing Output

Laser cutters can produce remarkable items with speed and accuracy. Architects use the machine to create models of their

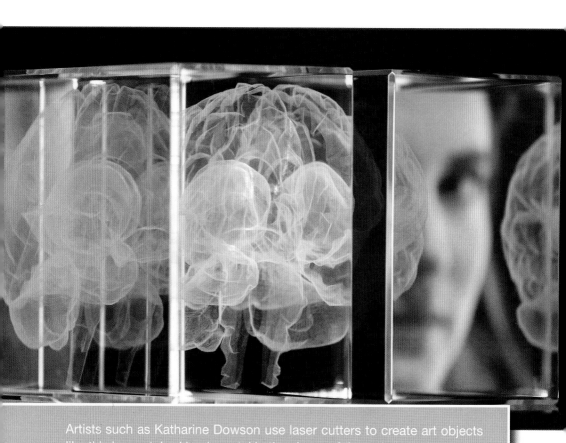

Artists such as Katharine Dowson use laser cutters to create art objects like this laser etched lead crystal in the shape of the artist's brain, copied from her own Magnetic Resonance Imaging (MRI) medical scan.

designs. The laser works with the same, or close to the same, materials that will be used in the finished structure. It also lets architects make quick design changes to one part of the building without having to build an entirely new model.

Lamp makers cut out interesting shapes from lampshades. And because lasers can cut through many materials—often several different ones at the same time—they are helpful in furniture design.

Artists and art students also turn to the laser cutter for their two- and three-dimensional projects. The machine lets artists have more control than with other tools as they experiment with different materials. Artists can also add color to their projects. They use their talents and skills to create designs, and then let the laser cutter etch or cut out their visions.

Chapter **FIVE**

YOUR PROJECT

Would you like to use a laser cutter to make a gift for Mother's Day, Valentine's Day, or someone's birthday? Want to make something for your own use? To sell? Or do you just want to try out a laser cutter?

A laser cutter project starts with an idea. Think about your interests. How do they relate to a project you'd like to do? Do you like to read? Make some bookmarks. Planning a party? Create your own invitations and decorations. Do you play chess? Make your own acrylic chess set. Are you a Jenga addict? Engrave the wooden blocks with your favorite images or sayings.

You may already know what you'd like to make. But if you're looking for inspiration, surf the web for ideas. Such sites as the Epilog Laser Sample Club, Thingiverse, Pinterest, Good Empire, and YouTube feature hundreds of ideas, demonstrations, and downloadable files for laser projects.

Laser projects start with your imagination. You can also find ideas on the internet. Next consider other factors. What is it? What is it made of? How long will it take? What will it cost?

Imagine your product before you begin. This exercise will help you choose the material you want to use. For a rustic look, choose wood. For a modern look, consider glass, metal, or acrylic. Once you have a good idea of what you're aiming for, you'll be able to make good decisions about which materials and which design elements contribute to your goals.

If you're making something with several parts, pay attention to scale. Scale is the size of a drawing of something compared to the size of the actual object. Consider how small some of the parts will be. If they're too small, they might break off. In the design process, zoom in and out of the design until it's the same size as the finished product will be. Also think about the material you plan to use. If your design allows for the possibility of tiny parts snapping off, redesign them.

Time and Money

Consider time: simple projects take less time; complex ones take more. For example, you can engrave an aluminum travel mug in about seven minutes. Cutting a piece of wood that measures 24 inches by 12 inches (61 cm by 30.5 cm) takes between 20 and 45 minutes, and that's just the time to actually cut or engrave the items.

You also need time to choose your design and obtain the right materials. And you may have to wait for your turn on the laser cutter. If you want to make something for a special occasion,

You can use a laser cutter for both two-dimensional and three-dimensional items such as this cube designed and fabricated at the Vinn:Lab at the technical college in Wildau, Germany.

give yourself plenty of lead time. Allow extra time for mistakes and do-overs. The first time you try to make something, it might not meet your expectations. You may need several tries to get a result you're happy with.

What's your budget? Material costs vary widely. You can buy a 6-inch by 24-inch (15-cm by 61-cm) sheet of one-quarter-inch- (0.63-cm-) thick basswood for around $10 at art, craft, and hobby retailers. A 12-inch by 12-inch (30.5-cm by 30.5-cm) piece of one-eighth-inch- (0.32-cm-) thick ABS plastic costs about the same. A ready-made bamboo tissue box runs about $20. A set of natural Brazilian agate slices with 18K gold trim will cost a lot more. A well-sized mahogany serving tray might go for more than $350. If you choose a relatively expensive material, consider making a prototype out of a cheaper material first. A prototype is an original model of an item used as a sample that can be copied or adjusted to create future designs.

Keep in mind that creating a prototype in a Fab Lab is perfectly fine. However, if you plan to produce many copies of the item, you will be crossing into a gray area of a Fab Lab's purpose. If you're making jewelry for friends, you're probably OK. But if you're trying to make lots of items to sell to raise money for college, buy a car, or even to donate to a charitable cause, you're engaging in "production." Fab Labs are designed as educational environments, not personal factories. If you want to pursue a profitable business, think about investing in your own laser cutter.

Several manufacturers offer new desktop laser cutters for sale between about $1,500 and $5,000. You can find laser cutters for sale directly from manufacturers. Before you buy, do some research and talk with your Fab Lab technician for advice about which features are most important to you. You can find

Using a laser cutter involves computer skills combined with knowledge of machinery operation. You can learn these skills in a Fab Lab. You don't need to know them before your first visit.

used machines as well, but buyer beware. Be sure to check out the laser cutter before you pay for it.

Tips for Successful Projects

Here are some tips from experienced laser cutters to help make your own project successful:

- To avoid smoke stains on engraved edges, especially on wood or leather, use masking tape to protect the surface. (You may need to increase the power a little as a result.) Peel off the tape when the engraving is complete.

- The grain in natural wood comes from the tree rings. The rings come from different growing patterns over a season or year. Darker grain is harder than light grain. Therefore, when you engrave natural wood, you'll see a striped pattern in the finished design. If you want a more uniform look, use laser plywood instead of natural wood.

- If your finished product needs to be painted, then plan to paint before you cut. That will keep grooves free of paint that might creep into the groove if you wait to paint until after engraving.

- If you're engraving a material with a thin wood veneer on top, be sure to engrave deep enough that the laser burns all the way through the veneer. If not, you'll end up with an uneven mixture of the veneer and whatever is below it.

- Cutting multiple parts of the same shape is easier if you can butt them up against each other. If you draw two squares using four lines for each square, the laser will see (and make) two cuts on the shared line, risking a burn. Instead, make the first square with four lines, but the second square with only three—share the fourth line with the first square.

- If you want to engrave a design that has mostly lines, you can use the raster setting, but using the vector setting will be much faster. Adjust to use lower power and higher speed than in raster mode.

- For extra sharpness when engraving, you can create a thin line around the edges of the cut. This is a nice effect for letters and words or other shapes. Make your image in a vector file and set the laser for vector cut. Use low power and fast speed to keep the laser from cutting all the way through the edge. The resulting thin line highlights the image.

- Make more of the same thing all at the same time. Suppose you want to make dozens of bookmarks engraved with the same image. Instead of making them one at a time, lay out a bunch of them at once. The laser can engrave them all in one cut. Make a vector file the size of the laser bed, and copy and paste as many items as you can fit into that space.

Try not to be too disappointed if your first laser cutting projects turn out less than perfect. Keep trying. Experiment with different materials and different power, speed, and frequency settings. When you get an outcome you're happy with, record the materials and settings you used for future reference. As you gain expertise, you can try more complex designs for even better results.

Chapter
SIX

FAB LABS AND YOUR FUTURE

Participating in a Fab Lab and learning to use a laser cutter and other equipment might be a fun experience, but it can also lead to more. For instance, you'll be able to apply what you've learned in a hands-on, practical way, with a finished product to show for it. You'll have the satisfaction of making something from scratch, which is at the heart of the Fab Lab concept.

You'll make connections both in the real world and with classroom subjects such as science, technology, engineering, arts and design, and mathematics. You'll also see more possibilities in the world around you. You might even come up with ideas for new inventions.

Being part of a Fab Lab is an activity you can include in job applications and college entrance essays. The experience reflects well-rounded interests beyond the classroom and says you're willing to take on new challenges.

When applying for a job, include your Fab Lab experience on the application to show your potential employer that you have extracurricular interests and like to try new things.

Using a laser cutter could even become an enjoyable, ongoing hobby. You can personalize your possessions and make your own gifts for others. You'll have a new way to meet others with similar interests. You may even serve as a volunteer or paid employee at a Fab Lab in the future.

Founding a Small Business

With proficiency in using a laser cutter, consider creating your own small business. You could make jewelry and sell it to friends, online, or in craft shows. For example, online marketplaces such as Etsy.com offer individuals a venue to sell items such as clothing, accessories, jewelry, home décor, invitations, and party decorations. You can sell your products ready-made or offer to customize or personalize them.

Another small business idea is to offer laser cutting services to others. Again, you can offer standard products or offer personalized and customized versions. Websites for several such companies are already posted. Search online for examples. You could also sell designs for laser projects to fellow Fab Lab participants.

Many established small businesses use laser cutting; for example, engravers use metal, wood, and acrylic to customize

Wrecords, a small business in New York City, uses a laser cutter to cut out designs from old vinyl records that the owner finds in used record stores, flea markets, and estate sales.

trophies, medals, plaques, and other awards. These companies are particularly appealing to sports teams for tournaments and end-of-the-year awards and for businesses looking to recognize

YOUFAB GLOBAL CREATIVE AWARDS

YouFab Global Creative Awards annually recognize the creativity of digital fabrication around the world. Entries are accepted from all types of Fab Lab machinery. Several laser cutting projects were recognized at the 2015 awards, including the following:

- The 2015 Judges' Special Prize went to Yuriko Wada of Japan for "Papertype," moveable type for printing made from laser-cut paper.
- Finalists Varvara and Mar from Estonia created "Circular Knitic," a knitting machine made with a 3D printer and laser cutter.
- In the art category, Ryo Kishi, of Japan, was a finalist with "atOms," a kinetic structure that suspends balls using streams of air. The parts were fabricated using a laser cutter.
- Another finalist in the art category came from Arthur Baude, of France, who made "Brumascope" in the Petit Fablab de Paris, one of the first Fab Labs in Paris. It generates images on a mist cloud accompanied by music. He designed the structure using Illustrator and cut it with a laser cutter.

sales representatives and employees of the month. You may be able to find a job in this environment, or see if a local business might take you on as an intern to learn the ropes.

If you're an artist, you can create two-dimensional art as well as three-dimensional sculptures for sale. You could even open your own gallery some day.

STEM/STEAM Education

Perhaps the best use for skills learned in a Fab Lab is in the workforce. Despite concerns about overall unemployment in the United States, leaders are also worried about a future lack of skilled workers. According to *Occupational Outlook Quarterly*, a publication of the U.S. Bureau of Labor Statistics, by 2022 the nation will need nearly nine million workers in fields related to science, technology, engineering, arts/design, and mathematics. In manufacturing alone, six hundred thousand jobs will exist by 2018 without people with the skills to fill them. Fewer than 50 percent of those jobs will require college degrees. The trouble is too few young adults are pursuing education in those abilities.

As early as 1957, when the Soviet Union beat the United States into space with the launch of the Sputnik satellite, leaders became aware of a need to educate students in the fields of engineering and technology. President Dwight D. Eisenhower called on the nation to produce more scientists. He said the country needed "thousands more than we are now planning to have." The Space Race inspired students to enter the fields of science and engineering.

However, by the 1990s the need for these skilled workers had continued to increase. During that decade, educators brought together the fields of science, technology, engineering, and mathematics with a concept called STEM education. They found that skills taught in these subjects tended to work together in real-life jobs, so STEM called for integration of these subjects, teaching them together rather than as separate units. Hands-on projects using these skills were encouraged.

In 2009, President Obama's budget called for $2.5 billion in additional federal funding for the National Science Foundation. It was the highest amount devoted to research and innovation in the nation's history. Some of the money went to encourage STEM education programs and recruit and train 100,000 new STEM teachers.

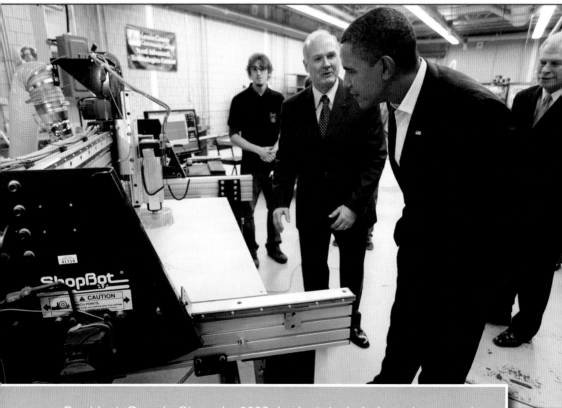

President Barack Obama's 2009 budget included an increase in funding for research and innovation and to encourage students to study science, technology, engineering, art and design, and mathematics.

Soon after, teachers and leaders in the fields of art and design began efforts to add an "A" to the STEM acronym to represent their fields. In perhaps the first "official" recognition of the new acronym, Elmo, one of the stars of the American children's television series *Sesame Street* replaced "STEM" with "STEAM" during the show's 2012–2013 season.

Fab Labs contribute to efforts to provide STEAM education, not only to students but also to adults in the community. They combine art and design with science, technology, engineering, and math in a fun way that encourages creativity through making. Creativity adds an important element to innovation. It brings STEAM skills together in a fun way, coordinating activities of the mind, eye, and hand.

Career Planning

When you work in a Fab Lab, you're exposed to the kinds of skills employers need. America's employers are begging for employees with STEAM skills to compete in the global economy. According to the U.S. Bureau of Labor Relations, by 2018 the following percentages of STEAM-related jobs will be in these fields:

- Computing: 71 percent
- Engineering: 16 percent
- Physical sciences: 7 percent
- Life sciences: 4 percent
- Mathematics: 2 percent

Applicants for more than half of these jobs will not need higher education. However, those who have a bachelor's degree or higher in a STEAM field can expect 26 percent higher pay

STEAM CAREERS

Job openings that use STEAM skills are increasing, but the labor supply is not. If you enjoy working in a Fab Lab, consider one or more of these potential careers:

- Aerospace engineer
- Agricultural and food science technician
- Architectural drafter
- Chemical technician
- Conservation scientist
- Computer and information research scientist
- Education, training, and library worker
- Electrical/electronics engineering technician
- Environmental science and protection
- Forensic science technician
- Forester
- Industrial engineer
- Life, physical, or social science technician
- Manufacturing factory worker
- Materials engineer
- Sales representative for manufacturing, technical, and scientific products
- Software developer
- Soil and plant scientist
- Surveying and mapping technician

for entry-level jobs than those in non-STEAM fields. And there will be 2.5 job openings in STEAM jobs for every one in a non-STEAM area.

Germany is experiencing similar shortages of skilled workers. They need more than 200,000 STEAM workers. And, according to the Royal Academy of Engineering, the United Kingdom will need 100,000 new STEAM majors every year between now and 2020 to fill anticipated jobs. That's one big reason why Fab Labs are thriving all over the world.

Glossary

ABS (acrylonitrile-butadiene-styrene) An inexpensive engineering plastic.

additive process A manufacturing process that creates an object by adding layer upon layer of the design.

anodizing A process used to coat such metals as aluminum to protect the finish before laser cutting.

computer-aided design (CAD) The use of computer software to create an automated process for two-dimensional or three-dimensional design.

computer numerical control (CNC) A type of machine tool controlled by computers.

laser Light amplification by stimulated emission of radiation.

laser cutter A computer-guided machine that uses an intense beam of light to cut or engrave a piece of wood, acrylic, fabric, rubber, leather, or other material.

milling machine A computer-guided machine that cuts away material, particularly wood, steel, and other metals.

monogram A design combining two or more letters, usually a person's initials.

personal digital fabrication A type of manufacturing by individuals that uses computer-controlled machines to produce objects.

polycarbonate A strong, heat-resistant synthetic resin.

prototype An original model of an item used as a sample that can be copied or used to create future designs.

PVC (polyvinyl chloride) A synthetic plastic polymer, an inorganic material used as plastic and resin.

raster A cutting technique used with a laser cutter that works like an inkjet printer to engrave objects.

resonator A device that moves electromagnetic radiation back and forth.

router A power tool guided by a computer file that is commonly used in carpentry for making grooves in wood for joints and moldings.

scale The size of a drawing of something compared to the size of the actual object.

3D printer A printer that produces a computer-generated object by adding layers until the object is complete.

vector A cutting technique used on a laser cutter to cut things out.

vinyl cutter A computer-controlled machine with a sharp blade used to cut out shapes from thin sheets of plastic.

Association of Professional Model Makers
(APMM)
P.O. Box 165
Hamilton, NY 13346
(315) 750-0803
Website: http://www.modelmakers.org/home
APMM is an organization of professional model makers that
offers communication, education, and resource connection
with leading-edge technology.

Consumer Technology Association (CTA)
1919 South Eads Street
Arlington, VA 22202
(703) 907-7650
Website: http://www.cta.tech
The Consumer Technology Association is an organization for
companies in the consumer technology industry. It offers
market research, networking opportunities, training, and
promotional programs.

The Fab Foundation
50 Milk Street, 16th Floor
Boston, MA 02109
(857) 333-7777
Website: http://www.fabfoundation.org
The Fab Foundation is a nonprofit organization that grew out of
the Massachusetts Institute of Technology's Center for Bits
and Atoms Fab Lab Program. It provides access for
community organizations and schools to tools, information,
and financial means to use digital fabrication to create
opportunities to improve lives .

International Society for Technology in Education (ISTE)
1530 Wilson Boulevard, Suite 730
Arlington, VA 22209
(703) 348-4784
Website: http://www.iste.org
ISTE is a nonprofit organization of educators dedicated to using
digital strategies to improve teaching and learning in a
technology-powered world.

Laser Institute of America (LIA)
13501 Ingenuity Drive, Suite 128
Orlando, FL 32826
(800) 345-2737
Website: https://www.lia.org/index.php
LIA is an international society that works to encourage use of
lasers in a variety of applications. Its main focus is laser safety.

Society of Manufacturing Engineers Canada (SME)
7100 Woodbine Avenue, Suite 312
Markham, ON L3R 5J2
Canada
(888) 322-7333
Website: http://www.sme.org
SME Canada is an organization that connects engineers,
technologists, technicians, and others involved in
manufacturing and seeks to prepare workers for the
technology of the future.

United States Fab Lab Network
2320 Renaissance Boulevard
Sturtevant, WI 53177

(262) 898-7430

Website: http://usfln.org

The United States Fab Lab Network is a group of Fab Labs that exchange information and resources to encourage people to experiment and invent new products.

UnLondon Digital Media Association

211 King Street

London, ON N6A 1C9

Canada

(226) 271-4753

Website: http://www.unlondon.ca

Describing itself as "Art + Make + Tech," UnLondon Digital Media Association provides digital literacy education, an "UnLab" makerspace, workshops, and more to encourage use of digital technology.

Websites

Because of the changing nature of internet links, Rosen Publishing has developed an online list of websites related to the subject of this book. This site is updated regularly. Please use this link to access the list:

http://www.rosenlinks.com/GCFL/laser

Aliverti, Paolo. *The Maker's Manual: A Practical Guide to the New Industrial Revolution.* San Francisco, CA: Maker Media Inc., 2015.

Anderson, Chris. *The New Industrial Revolution.* New York, NY: Crown Business, 2012.

Au, Jesse Harrington, and Emily Gertz. *3D CAD with Autodesk 123D: Designing for 3D Printing, Laser Cutting, and Personal Fabrication.* San Francisco, CA: Maker Media, 2016.

Baker, Laura Berens. *Laser Cutting for Fashion and Textiles Hardcover.* London, England: Laurence King Publishing LTD, 2016.

Bow, James. *Lasers.* New York, NY: Gareth Stevens Publishing, 2016.

Brezina, Corona. *Top STEM Careers in Math.* New York, NY: Rosen Publishing, 2015.

Cantor, Doug. *The Big Book of Hacks.* San Francisco, CA: Weldon Owen Inc., 2016.

Cline, Lydia. *3D Printing and CNC Fabrication with SketchUp.* New York, NY: McGraw-Hill Education, 2016.

Ford, Edward. *Getting Started with CNC.* San Francisco, CA: Maker Media, 2016.

Goodwin, Peter. *3D Printing Unleashed: 7 Key Questions Answered Inside.* London, England: Artbot Ltd., 2015.

Hagler, Gina. *Top STEM Careers in Engineering.* New York, NY: Rosen Publishing, 2015.

Hausman, Kalani Kirk, and Richard Horne. *3D Printing For Dummies.* Hoboken, NJ: John Wiley & Sons, Inc., 2014.

Kaplan, Jack. *Getting Started with 3D Carving.* San Francisco, CA: Maker Media, 2016.

Kemp, Adam. *The Makerspace Workbench.* San Francisco, CA: Maker Media, 2013.

Kloski, Liza Wallach, and Nick Kloski. *Getting Started with 3D Printing: A Hands-on Guide to the Hardware, Software, and Services Behind the New Manufacturing Revolution.* San Francisco, CA: Maker Media, 2016.

La Bella, Laura. *Top STEM Careers in Technology*. New York, NY: Rosen Publishing, 2015.

Leavitt, Amie Jane. *Physical Computing and Makerspaces*. New York, NY: Rosen Central, 2015.

Lefteri, Chris. *Making It: Manufacturing Techniques for Product Design.* London, England: Laurence King Publishing LTD, 2012.

Petrikowski, Nicki Peter. *Getting the Most Out of Makerspaces to Create with 3-D Printers*. New York, NY: Rosen Publishing, 2015.

Shea, Therese. *Getting the Most Out of Makerspaces to Go from Idea to Market*. New York, NY: Rosen Publishing, 2015.

Suen, Anastasia. *Top STEM Careers in Science*. New York, NY: Rosen Publishing, 2015.

Bibliography

"American Recovery and Reinvestment Act of 2009, Public Law No. 111-16." February 17, 2009 (http://www.thomas.gov/home/h1/Recovery_Bill_Div_A.pdf).

Cavalcanti, Gui. "Is it a Hackerspace, Makerspace, TechShop, or FabLab?" Makezine.com, May 22, 2013 (http://makezine.com/2013/05/22/the-difference-between-hackerspaces-makerspaces-techshops-and-fablabs/).

Chunkman, Stump. "How to Use a Laser Cutter." Instructables.com, 2016 (http://www.instructables.com/id/How-to-Use-a-Laser-Cutter/).

"5 Key CNC Machines in a Fab Lab." MakingSociety.com, January 19, 2013 (http://makingsociety.com/2013/01/5-key-cnc-machines-in-fab-lab/).

Ford, Richard. "EU Ruling Clears Up the Future of Fruit Lasering." *Grocer*, June 17, 2013 (http://www.thegrocer.co.uk/buying-and-supplying/categories/fresh/eu-ruling-clears-up-the-future-of-fruit-lasering/344198.article?redirCanon=1).

Gershenfeld, Neil. "Unleash your creativity in a Fab Lab." TED.com, February 2007 (https://www.ted.com/talks/neil_gershenfeld_on_fab_labs/transcript?language=en).

Hom, Elaine J. "What is STEM Education?" LiveScience.com, February 11, 2014 (http://www.livescience.com/43296-what-is-stem-education.html).

"How Does Laser Cutting Work?" ESAB Knowledge Center, July 29, 2013 (http://www.esabna.com/us/en/education/blog/how-does-laser-cutting-work.cfm).

Isaac-Goizé, Tina. "Pre-Fall 2016, John Galliano." *Vogue*, January 27, 2016 (http://www.vogue.com/fashion-shows/

pre-fall-2016/john-galliano).

"Laser Cutting Safety." Carnegie Mellon University. Retrieved May 14, 2016 (https://www.cmu.edu/ehs/fact-sheets/laser-cutter-safety.pdf).

Mattern, Steven. "Tutorial: Laser Cutting Techniques and Projects." *Make:*, October 23, 2013 (http://makezine.com/2013/10/23/tutorial-laser-cutting-techniques-and-projects/).

Noe, Rain. "Laser-Etched Fruit May Not be Good for You, but It's Happening in the EU." *Core 77*, June 25, 2013 (http://www.core77.com/posts/25106/Laser-Etched-Fruit-May-Not-be-Good-for-You-but-Its-Happening-in-the-EU).

Phelps, Nicole. "Spring 2011 Ready-to-Wear Jean Paul Gaultier." Vogue, October 1, 2010 (http://www.vogue.com/fashion-shows/spring-2011-ready-to-wear/jean-paul-gaultier).

"Sample Club: Downloadable Files for Your Epilog Laser." EpilogLaser.com, 2015 (https://www.epiloglaser.com/resources/sample-club.htm).

"Stem 101: Intro to tomorrow's jobs." U.S. Bureau of Labor Statistics, 2014 (http://www.bls.gov/careeroutlook/2014/spring/art01.pdf).

"10 Tips and Tricks for Laser Engraving and Cutting." Instructables.com, 2016 (http://www.instructables.com/id/10-Tips-and-Tricks-for-Laser-Engraving-and-Cutting/).

Travis. "Laser Art is on a Whole Different Level." (Video) TheChive, June 8, 2015 (http://thechive.com/2015/06/08/laser-art-is-on-a-whole-different-level-video/).

"What is a Fab Lab?" YouTube, June 24, 2013 (https://www.youtube.com/watch?v=IPF7zDSf-LA).

Williams-Alvarez, Jennifer. "What you need to know about laser-cut clothing." Engadge.com, June 17, 2014 (http://www.engadget.com/2014/06/17/laser-cut-clothing-explainer/).

Young, David. "Cooking Dinner and Project Oasis," *Inventing Interactive*, July 2, 2010 (http://www.inventinginteractive.com/about/).

Index

About the Author

Mary-Lane Kamberg is a professional writer and the author of more than twenty-five nonfiction books for young readers. She lives in the Kansas City suburb of Olathe, Kansas. She toured the Fab Lab on the Business and Technology Campus at Metropolitan Community College in Kansas City, Missouri, when writing this book.

Photo Credits

Designer: Nicole Russo; Editor: Carolyn DeCarlo;
Photo Researcher: Nicole DiMella